Dinosaur Babies

by Kathleen Weidner Zoehfeld ▪ illustrated by Lucia Washburn

HarperCollinsPublishers

To C.B.O.
—K.W.Z.

To Megan
—L.W.

Special thanks to Dr. John R. Horner,
Curator of The Museum of The Rockies at Montana State University,
for his time and expert review

The *Let's-Read-and-Find-Out Science* book series was originated by Dr. Franklyn M. Branley, Astronomer Emeritus and former Chairman of the American Museum–Hayden Planetarium, and was formerly co-edited by him and Dr. Roma Gans, Professor Emeritus of Childhood Education, Teachers College, Columbia University. Text and illustrations for each of the books in the series are checked for accuracy by an expert in the relevant field. For more information about Let's-Read-and-Find-Out Science books, write to HarperCollins Children's Books, 10 East 53rd Street, New York, NY 10022.

HarperCollins®, ☂®, and Let's Read-and-Find-Out Science® are trademarks of HarperCollins Publishers Inc.

DINOSAUR BABIES
Text copyright © 1999 by Kathleen Weidner Zoehfeld
Illustrations copyright © 1999 by Lucia Washburn
For information address HarperCollins Children's Books, a division of HarperCollins Publishers,
10 East 53rd Street, New York, NY 10022. http://www.harperchildrens.com

Library of Congress Cataloging-in-Publication Data
Zoehfeld, Kathleen Weidner.
   Dinosaur babies / by Kathleen Weidner Zoehfeld ; illustrated by Lucia Washburn.
      p.   cm. — (Let's-read-and-find-out science. Stage 2)
   Summary: Describes the parenting habits of the Maiasaura, a dinosaur whose way of raising children bore similarities to that of birds.
   ISBN 0-06-027141-8. — ISBN 0-06-027142-6 (lib. bdg.) — ISBN 0-06-445162-3 (pbk.)
   1. Dinosaurs—Infancy—Juvenile literature. [1. Maiasaura. 2. Dinosaurs. 3. Animals—Infancy.] I. Washburn, Lucia, ill. II. Title.
III. Series.
QE862.D5Z64   1999   98-43594
567.9—dc21   CIP
                                                                                                                    AC

Typography by Elynn Cohen
1 2 3 4 5 6 7 8 9 10
❖
First Edition

Dinosaur Babies

Inside her egg, the tiny dinosaur baby squirmed.

She bumped the eggshell with her snout, and her egg began to crack.

She pushed with her legs.

The top of the egg popped open, and she wriggled out.

Bits of damp eggshell stuck to her head.

She shook herself and toppled over on her chin.

She was a maiasaur, born more than 70 million years ago. What was life like for a baby maiasaur, or for any baby dinosaur?

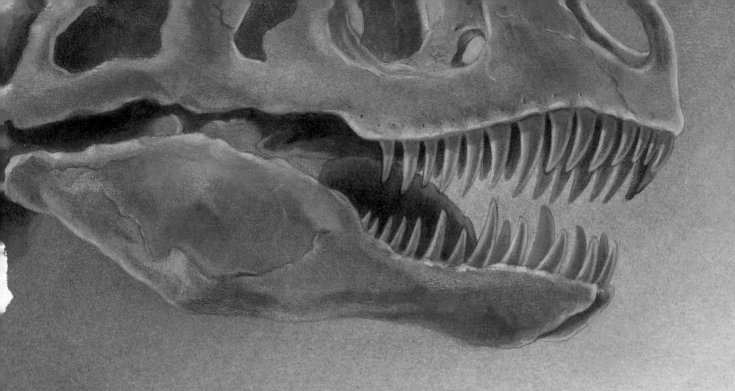

Most of the dinosaur skeletons we see in the museum are huge.
Imagine a dinosaur baby small enough to hold in your arms.
What would happen to this tiny creature in a world of giants?
Was she left to fend for herself? Or did her gigantic parents take
care of her?

It is hard to tell what kind of parents dinosaurs were. Fossils tell
us almost everything we know about dinosaurs. But for most types
of dinosaurs, fossils are scarce.

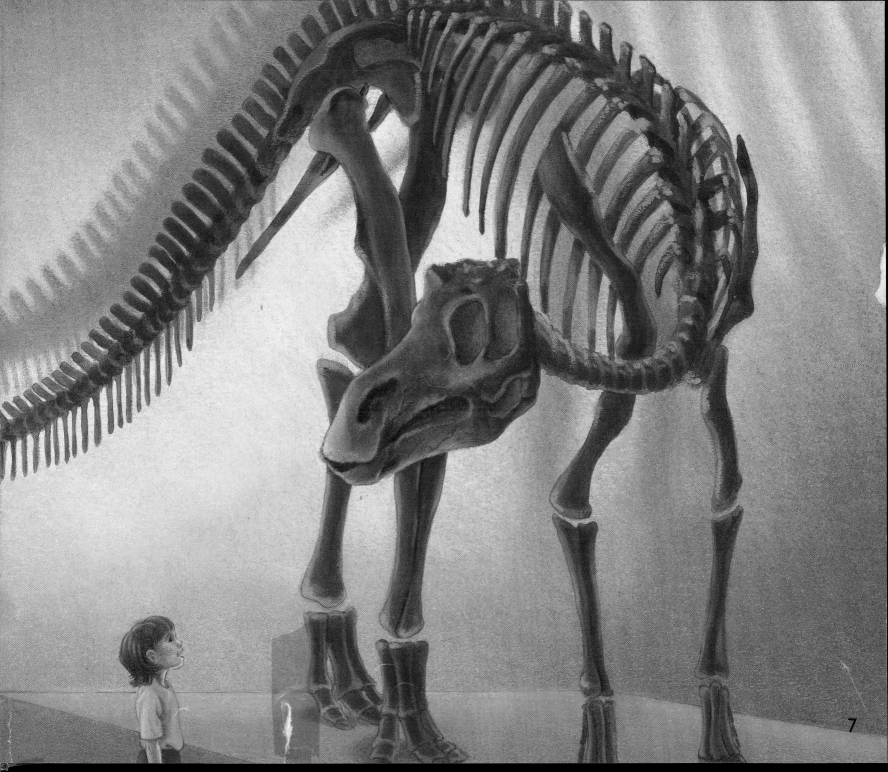

Some animals alive today are related to, or are similar to, dinosaurs. When fossils are few, scientists often study living dinosaur relatives. These animals can help us understand how dinosaurs might have behaved.

The lizards, turtles, and crocodiles of today are reptiles. Dinosaurs were reptiles, too. Most reptiles lay hard-shelled eggs.

We wouldn't call lizards
and turtles the greatest parents.
They lay their eggs and forget
about them. When the babies
hatch, they are on their own.
Maybe some dinosaurs were
like lizard parents.

But, of all the reptiles, dinosaurs
are most closely related to crocodiles.
Crocodiles make nests and fiercely
guard their eggs from enemies.

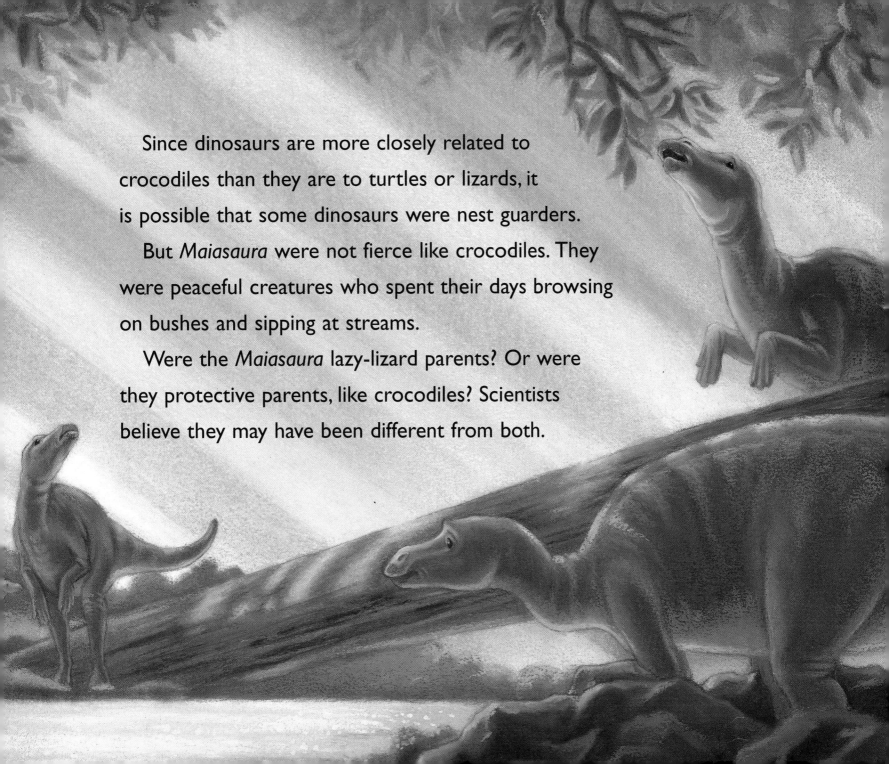

Since dinosaurs are more closely related to crocodiles than they are to turtles or lizards, it is possible that some dinosaurs were nest guarders.

But *Maiasaura* were not fierce like crocodiles. They were peaceful creatures who spent their days browsing on bushes and sipping at streams.

Were the *Maiasaura* lazy-lizard parents? Or were they protective parents, like crocodiles? Scientists believe they may have been different from both.

Birds of today are also related to dinosaurs. Like reptiles, all birds lay hard-shelled eggs.

Most birds are careful parents. Not only do they build nests and protect their eggs, they also feed and watch over their babies until they are old enough to leave the nest. Scientists believe that some dinosaurs might have behaved like bird parents. For *Maiasaura*, an amazing number of fossil clues help to prove they did.

In Montana, scientists discovered a group of ancient *Maiasaura* nests, filled with fossil eggs and babies. Near the nests were the bones of an adult maiasaur. (The name *Maiasaura* comes from Greek words meaning "good mother lizard.")

The fossils tell us that a baby maiasaur started her life inside a small oval egg. The eggs of her brothers and sisters surrounded her in the great hollowed-out mound that was their nest.

When the baby hatched, she was small and scrawny. She was hungry, but her legs were wobbly. She could not toddle out of the nest on her own. Like baby birds, she and her newly hatched brothers and sisters probably squawked for their mother.

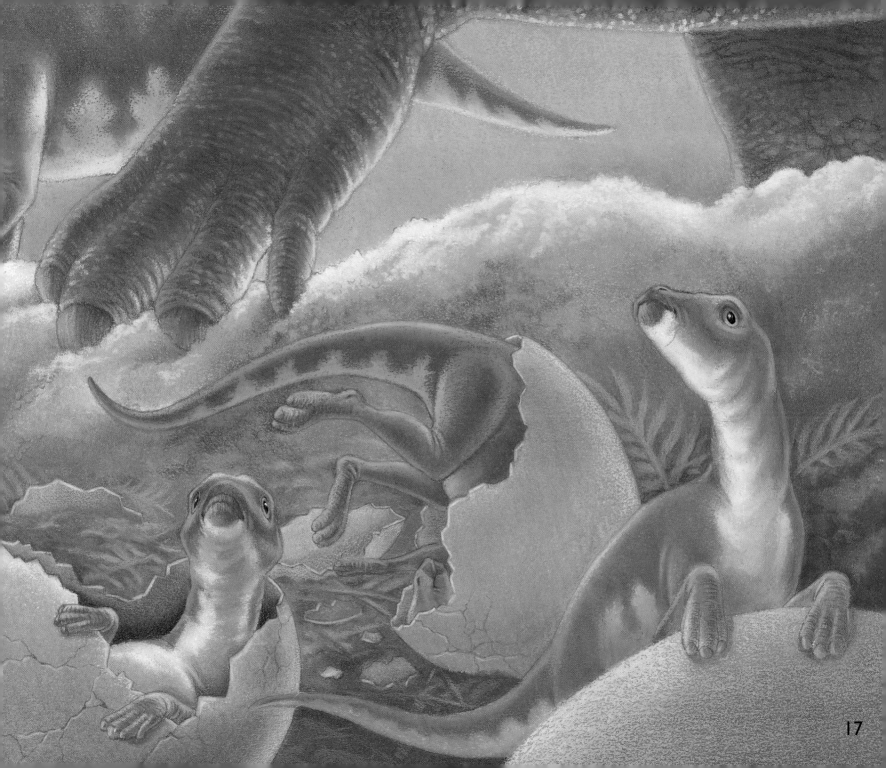

17

And what a huge mother she was! The newborns were about 18 inches long—that's about how long you were when you were born. Their mother was nearly the size of a school bus. Her enormous head loomed over the edge of the nest. But her babies were not scared.

She held sweet berries in her mouth. The babies scrambled toward her and gobbled up the berries. Then they probably hunched together and fell asleep. While they slept, at least one grown-up stayed near the nest to protect them.

Small, deadly, meat-eating dinosaurs called *Troodon* may have prowled the nesting grounds in packs. If *Troodon* were allowed to raid the nests, many babies would be carried away for *Troodon* snacks. *Maiasaura* parents were watchful. If a troodon attacked, a maiasaur could stomp on it with its huge hind legs.

When a maiasaur baby was big and strong enough, she would follow her mother out of the nest. Fossils tell us that a young maiasaur may have stayed with her parents for many years.

Not far from the nesting grounds, scientists found a vast area covered in *Maiasaura* bones. Some of the bones belonged to youngsters and some to adults.

Scientists believe that these are the remains of a *Maiasaura* herd. The adults in the herd would have protected the youngsters from the ferocious tyrannosaurs, called *Albertosaurus*, that stalked the area. Sadly, the members of this particular herd must have died all at once, when a volcano erupted, spewing hot ash and deadly fumes.

Today, many types of birds gather together in nesting grounds, much like the *Maiasaura*'s. And some travel in flocks, much like the *Maiasaura* herds.

We know that bird eggs need to be kept warm so they can hatch. Most birds sit on their eggs to keep them warm. Dinosaur eggs needed to be kept warm, too. But the 4,000-pound maiasaur moms could never have sat on their eggs. If they had, the eggs would surely have been crushed!

Bits of fossilized plants in the nests hint that perhaps maiasaurs covered the eggs with leaves and branches. As the leaves rotted, they would have warmed the eggs.

Smaller, leaner dinosaurs such as *Troodon* and *Oviraptor* may have sat on their nests to hatch their eggs the way birds do.

In the dry country of Mongolia, scientists have found many nests and a few skeletons of the *Oviraptor*.

In some ways, the *Oviraptor* even looked like a bird. It had long legs, a toothless beak, and a crest on top of its head.

Oviraptor skeletons are very rare. Even so, three oviraptors have been found lying on top of their nests. Oviraptors must have stuck by their nests with great determination.

Whether oviraptors took care of their babies after they were hatched, no one is sure. But there is an interesting clue. Two tiny skulls of meat-eating dinosaurs were found in one of the oviraptor nests.

Did the mother oviraptor raid the nests of other dinosaurs, returning with the tiny babies to feed her own young? That is one possibility. Scientists hope that, as more fossils are found, we may be able to tell for sure.

Like lizards and turtles, some dinosaurs probably laid their eggs and never thought about them again.

But we now know that maiasaurs and oviraptors, and possibly many other types of dinosaurs, built nests and guarded them. And some dinosaurs must have fed and protected their babies for months, or even years. Life in the land of the giants may not have been as terrifying as we thought.

Next time you go to the museum, take a look at *Tyrannosaurus rex*. What kind of mom do you think she'd be? She may look pretty scary to you, but to her babies, she might have been as gentle as a bird.

MAKE A "FOSSIL" EGG

You will need:

1 egg
1 bowl
2 cups cold water
1 plastic spoon or stirring stick
4 cups plaster of Paris

$1/2$-gallon-size cardboard milk or
juice carton with the top cut off
baby powder
screwdriver
small paintbrush

1. Crack the egg carefully on the edge of the bowl. Dispose of the yolk and white so that you have two empty shell halves. Gently rinse them and set them aside to dry.
2. Pour 1 cup of water into the bowl. Stir in 2 cups plaster of Paris until smooth and creamy.
3. Pour the mixture into the bottom of the milk carton.
4. Sprinkle a layer of baby powder on the surface of the mixture in the milk carton.
5. Gently press eggshells side by side into the plaster until they're about half covered.
6. Let the plaster set for about 30 minutes.

7. Sprinkle more baby powder on top, covering the entire surface, including the shells and the plaster of Paris around them.
8. Repeat step 2 to make a new batch of plaster.
9. Pour the new plaster over the shells. Let the plaster harden for at least a day.
10. Tear the carton away from the hardened piece of plaster—your "rock." Look at your "rock" carefully. You should see two stripes where you sprinkled the baby powder.
11. Tap the screwdriver gently on the stripes. The plaster should fall away, revealing the eggshells. Carefully brush away the baby powder with the paintbrush.

Paleontologists have to be extremely careful when digging up fossils. Like these eggshells, real fossilized eggs are very fragile. As you excavate your fossil eggshells, take care! If you like, you can try making a sturdier fossil using a clean chicken bone instead of the eggshells.